NORTH KOREA

EXPLORE THE COUNTRIES

Big Buddy Books
An Imprint of Abdo Publishing
abdopublishing.com

Julie Murray

abdopublishing.com

Published by Abdo Publishing, a division of ABDO, PO Box 398166, Minneapolis, Minnesota 55439.
Copyright © 2016 by Abdo Consulting Group, Inc. International copyrights reserved in all countries. No part of this book may be reproduced in any form without written permission from the publisher. Big Buddy Books™ is a trademark and logo of Abdo Publishing.

Printed in the United States of America, North Mankato, Minnesota.
092015
012016

Cover Photo: Shutterstock.com.
Interior Photos: AFP/AFP/Getty Images (p. 31); AFP/Getty Images (p. 17); Raymond Cunningham/Getty
    Images (p. 11); DONG-A ILBO/AFP/Getty Images (p. 16); Jonas Gratzer/Getty Images (pp. 28, 35);
    Robert Harding/Glow Images (p. 5); Mark Edward Harris/Getty Images (p. 11); HOANG DINH NAM/
    AFP/Getty Images (p. 35); © iStockphoto.com (pp. 9, 25); Ed Jones/AFP/Getty Images (p. 19); Kyodo/AP
    Photo (pp. 33, 35); Eric LAFFORGUE/Getty Images (p. 34); Mondadori/Getty Images (p. 15);
    Shutterstock.com (pp. 13, 19, 21, 23, 27, 29, 37, 38); Sovfoto/Getty Images (p. 15); Xinhua/Alamy (p. 34).

Coordinating Series Editor: Megan M. Gunderson
Editor: Katie Lajiness
Contributing Editor: Marcia Zappa
Graphic Design: Adam Craven

Country population and area figures taken from the CIA World Factbook.

Library of Congress Cataloging-in-Publication Data

Murray, Julie, 1969-
  North Korea / Julie Murray.
      pages cm. -- (Explore the countries ; set 3)
  Includes index.
  ISBN 978-1-68078-069-7
  1. Korea (North)--Juvenile literature. I. Title.
  DS932.M86 2016
  951.93--dc23
                           2015027501

NORTH KOREA

CONTENTS

Around the World

Our world has many countries. Each country has beautiful land. It has its own rich history. And, the people have their own languages and ways of life.

North Korea is a country in Asia. What do you know about North Korea? Let's learn more about this place and its story!

Did You Know?

Korean is the official language of North Korea.

North Korea's leaders are honored throughout the country. They are featured in many paintings and monuments.

Passport to North Korea

North Korea is a country in East Asia. The country shares borders with China and Russia to the north. It borders South Korea to the south. North Korea borders the Sea of Japan to the east. The Korean Bay is to the west.

North Korea's total area is 46,540 square miles (120,538 sq km). Nearly 25 million people live there.

WHERE IN THE WORLD?

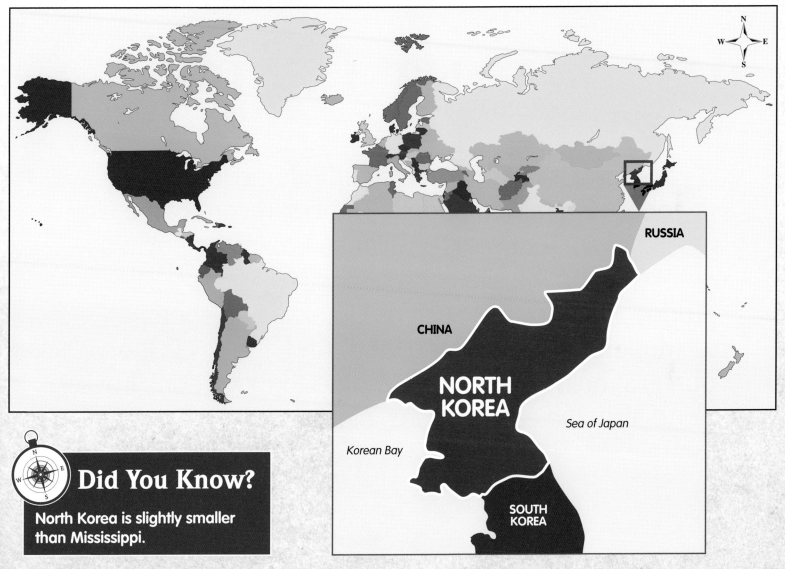

RUSSIA

CHINA

NORTH KOREA

Sea of Japan

Korean Bay

SOUTH KOREA

Did You Know?

North Korea is slightly smaller than Mississippi.

IMPORTANT CITIES

Pyongyang is North Korea's **capital** and largest city, with about 2.6 million people. The first record of the city was in 108 BC. That year, a Chinese trading colony was established on the site of an ancient city.

Today, many goods such as clothing and shoes are manufactured in Pyongyang. And, the city is the country's main travel center. Many North Koreans travel to and from the city by buses, planes, and trains.

SAY IT

Pyongyang
PYAWNG-YANG

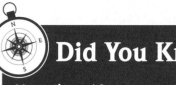

Did You Know?

More than 60 percent of North Koreans live in cities. In the United States and Canada, more than 80 percent of people live in cities.

Chongjin

NORTH KOREA

Hamhung

Pyongyang

The Arch of Triumph is one of the largest monuments in Pyongyang. It stands 197 feet (60 m) tall. The Arch honors North Korea's fight against Japan in the early 1900s.

Hamhung is another large North Korean city. It is home to more than 709,000 people. This port city serves as a center for North Korea's trade. Hamhung's factories make machines, metals, and foods.

Chongjin is also a major city in North Korea. About 615,000 people live there. It was once a small fishing village. Now, Chongjin is one of the country's top cities for manufacturing iron and steel.

SAY IT

Hamhung
HAHM-hung

Chongjin
CHAWNG-JIHN

The Hamhung Grand Theater is the largest theater in North Korea.

위대한령도자김정일동지만세!

Much of North Korea was destroyed during the Korean War in the 1950s. Chongjin was one of the places rebuilt by the government.

North Korea in History

About 5,000 years ago, people traveled from what is now China and Russia to the **peninsula** of Korea. Korea came together as one **dynasty** during AD 935. Koryo dynasty kings ruled until 1392.

During the 1800s, China, Japan, and Russia fought for authority over Korea. Korea was under Japanese rule from 1910 to 1945. Japanese rule was not easy. The Koreans had to speak Japanese and honor a Japanese faith.

Korea's final dynasty ended in 1910. Many works of art from Korea's dynasties remain.

Did You Know?

The name *Korea* came from the Koryo dynasty.

Japan ruled Korea until the end of **World War II**. Then, the United States and Russia took control of the land. Korea officially separated into North Korea and South Korea in 1948. In North Korea, the **Communists** took over farms, factories, and television stations, among other businesses.

North Korea wanted to make the Korean **peninsula** one whole country. So, North Korean troops attacked South Korea on June 25, 1950. More than 2.5 million people lost their lives during the Korean War. The war ended on July 27, 1953. No lasting peace agreement was ever reached.

Kim Il Sung was the first leader of North Korea. He ruled for 46 years until his death in 1994.

SAY IT

Kim Il Sung
KIHM-IHL-SUHNG

About 406,000 North Korean soldiers died during the Korean War.

TIMELINE

427

Pyongyang became the **capital** of the Koguryo kingdom. In 668, the city was taken by Chinese **invaders**.

1990s

Thousands of North Koreans died of hunger. Many crops could not grow because there were floods or too little rain.

1419–1450

King Sejong was head of the Choson **dynasty** for more than 30 years. He made a new, easy Korean alphabet. This alphabet helped Koreans learn to read and write.

1994

Kim Il Sung died on July 8. His son Kim Jong Il became North Korea's new leader.

SAY IT

Kim Jong Il
KIHM-JAWNG-IHL

2009

North Korea tested weapons and conducted powerful **nuclear** tests beneath the earth. Nearly every country on earth is against this type of testing.

2015

North Korea had a serious **drought**. Many wetlands used to grow rice dried up. Countries around the world gave money to provide food. However, millions of people still did not have enough food.

An Important Symbol

North Korea's flag was adopted in 1948. The blue stripes stand for peace. The white stripes stand for strength and honor. And, the red stripe stands for **Communism**.

North Korea is a Communist country. The leader of the Communist Party is the most powerful person in the country. He is the head of the government and the military.

Did You Know?

North Korea has one of the most uniform populations in the world. Nearly every person in the country is Korean.

North Korea's flag has a red star, which stands for Communism.

Kim Jong Un became the leader of North Korea in 2011.

SAY IT

Kim Jong Un
KIHM-JAWNG-UHN

ACROSS THE LAND

North Korea has mountains, valleys, and rivers. The Yalu River runs about 490 miles (790 km) through the country. It is North Korea's longest river. Mount Paektu is the country's highest mountain.

North Korea has two **monsoon** seasons. The winter winds bring dry, cold air. The summer winds bring hot, wet weather and heavy rains.

Did You Know?

In July, the average temperature in North Korea is 70°F (21°C) to 80°F (27°C). In January, the average temperature is about -5°F (-21°C) to 18°F (-9°C).

The Yalu River forms part of the border between North Korea and China.

Mount Paektu is 9,003 feet (2,744 m) high.

21

Earning a Living

The North Korean government controls the nation's schools, hospitals, factories, farms, and other businesses. Many North Koreans are factory workers. They produce cement, metal, machines, and other goods.

Some North Koreans work on farms or in mines. Rice is the biggest farm crop. Other crops include barley, corn, potatoes, and wheat. The area's **natural resources** include coal, iron ore, lead, and zinc.

Factories in North Korea make goods such as clothing, shoes, and watches.

LIFE IN NORTH KOREA

North Korea is known for being a private country. Many facts about this country are unknown. However, some things have been shared with the world.

Most North Koreans eat rice every day. They add fish and vegetables such as beans for taste. Meat is less common.

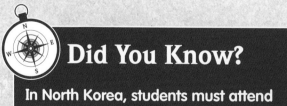

Did You Know?

In North Korea, students must attend school for 12 years.

Kimchi is popular in North Korea. There are many types of this spicy cabbage dish.

Some North Koreans practice tae kwon do, a style of fighting. Others do a kind of wrestling called *ssirum*.

The North Korean government does not support any faith. People are told to believe in their leaders.

North Koreans enjoy Western sports, such as basketball.

Did You Know?

The North Korean government controls radio, television, and newspapers. It bans any writing or art that does not agree with Communist ideas.

The Pohyon Temple is on Mount Myohyang. The government keeps temples open as part of Korean history.

FAMOUS FACES

North Korea's government has had three leaders since 1948. Kim Il Sung selected his son Kim Jong Il to lead after his death.

Kim Jong Il was born on February 16, 1941, in what is now Russia. He was the leader from 1994 to 2011.

Before Kim Jong Il, North Korea aimed to provide for itself. The country's leaders did not like depending on other governments. However, Kim Jong Il tried to mend ties with countries around the world.

Did You Know?

Kim Jong Il loved movies, and he helped make many films.

Kim Jong Il (*right*) was known for being a powerful and controlling leader.

Kim Jong Il died on December 17, 2011. His son Kim Jong Un then became leader.

Kim Jong Un was born on January 8. Many people believe he was born in 1983. His exact birth year is not known. As a young man, Kim Jong Un attended a Swiss school.

Kim Jong Un leads many government groups in North Korea. He is the first secretary of the Korean Workers' Party and chairman of the Central Military Commission. Kim Jong Un is also chairman of the National Defense Commission.

Kim Jong Un (*left*) is a big fan of basketball. He met American basketball player Dennis Rodman in 2013.

Tour Book

Imagine traveling to North Korea! Here are some places you could go and things you could do.

 Swim

Munsu Water Park opened in 2013. It has swimming pools and waterslides.

See

The Pyongyang Circus is a national act with **acrobats**. Some talented kids start training when they are younger than ten years old!

🧭 Listen

North Korea has a set of five **operas**. They were written to further **Communist** ideals. The shows are put on in North Korea and other Communist countries, such as China and Vietnam.

🧭 Dance

The Arirang Festival is an arts festival in Pyongyang. It runs from July to September. North Koreans make art to tell stories about their country.

🧭 Watch

Runga Theme Park is home to a dolphin aquarium. Watch the dolphins do tricks with their trainers!

A Great Country

The story of North Korea is important to our world. North Korea is a land of giant mountains and flowing rivers. It is a country of people faithful to their leader.

The people and places that make up North Korea offer something special. They help make the world a more beautiful, interesting place.

The Tower of the Juche Idea was completed in 1982 for Kim Il Sung's 70th birthday. It stands 560 feet (170 m) tall and is made of 25,550 blocks. Each block stands for a day in Kim Il Sung's life.

North Korea Up Close

Official Name: Democratic People's Republic of Korea

Flag:

Population (rank): 24,983,205
(July 2015 est.)
(50th most-populated country)

Total Area (rank): 46,540 square miles
(99th largest country)

Capital: Pyongyang

Official Language: Korean

Currency: Won

Form of Government: Communist state

National Anthem: "Aegukka"
(Patriotic Song)

IMPORTANT WORDS

acrobat one who performs gymnastic feats requiring skillful control of the body.

capital a city where government leaders meet.

Communist (KAHM-yuh-nihst) of or relating to a form of government in which all or most land and goods are owned by the state. They are then divided among the people based on need.

drought (DRAUT) a long period of dry weather.

dynasty (DEYE-nuh-stee) a powerful group or family that rules for a long time.

invader someone who enters a place, such as a country, in order to take it over by force.

monsoon a seasonal wind in southern Asia that sometimes brings heavy rain.

natural resources useful and valued supplies from nature.

nuclear a type of energy that uses atoms. Atoms are tiny particles that make up matter.

opera a play that is mostly sung, with costumes, scenery, acting, and music.

peninsula land that sticks out into the water and is connected to a larger piece of land.

World War II a war fought in Europe, Asia, and Africa from 1939 to 1945.

WEBSITES

To learn more about Explore the Countries, visit **booklinks.abdopublishing.com**. These links are routinely monitored and updated to provide the most current information available.

INDEX